D1244579

DETROIT PUBLIC LIBRARY

3 5674 00138303 4

APPLES ON A STICK

THE FOLKLORE OF BLACK CHILDREN

DETROIT PUBLIC LIBRARY

DUFFIELD BRANCH
2507 W. GRAND BLVD.
DETROIT, MICH. 48208

DATE DUE

OCT 09 1991

APPLES ON A STICK

THE FOLKLORE OF BLACK CHILDREN

COLLECTED AND EDITED BY
BARBARA MICHELS
BETTYE WHITE

ILLUSTRATED BY
JERRY PINKNEY

COWARD-MCCANN, INC.
New York

j808.1
A64

C.3

Text copyright © 1983 by Barbara Michels
and Bettye White
Illustrations copyright © 1983 by Jerry Pinkney

All rights reserved. This book, or parts thereof, may not be reproduced in any form without permission in writing from the publishers. Published simultaneously in Canada by General Publishing Co. Limited, Toronto.

Printed in the United States of America

Typographic design by Charlotte Staub

First Printing

Library of Congress Cataloging in Publication Data
Apples on a stick.
    Summary: A collection of playground rhymes, including jump rope rhymes, nonsense verses, taunts, and verses used in circle games and hand claps.
    1. Folk poetry, American—Texas—Houston. 2. Children's poetry, American—Texas—Houston. 3. Afro-American folklore—Texas—Houston. [1. American poetry—Afro-American authors] I. Michels, Barbara. II. White, Bettye. III. Pinkney, Jerry, ill. PS477.5.C45A66
      1983   398'.2'0899607641411   82-14385
                ISBN 0-698-20567-7

ACKNOWLEDGMENTS

The collection of playground poetry of black children is a joint project of St. James Episcopal Church and St. James School, Houston, Texas. We are grateful to many who from the beginning believed in the reality of this book. Those who served on the Advisory Board gave generously of their time and talents: John Biggers, June Holly, Beverly Lowry, Robert Patten, Bubbha Thomas, James Tucker, Craig Washington, and Pauline Watson. Funding for the folklore collection was made possible by a gift from Mr. and Mrs. Harris Masterson and a grant from the Cultural Arts Council of Houston.

PREFACE

Apples on a Stick was first a dream. There was faith in the voice of the child. There was the fear that, uncollected and unpublished, an authentic American voice would be denied its rightful heritage, that black children might never have the self-affirmation that comes with seeing themselves, their lore and their language, in print. But most of all, there was the hope that the voice of the black child might be shared with all children, that as we rejoice in our differences, we might know how much we have in common. *Apples on a Stick* is dedicated in thanksgiving to the many children of light and grace who opened to us, with enthusiasm and trust, the private world of children at play.

APPLES ON A STICK

THE FOLKLORE OF BLACK CHILDREN

Apples on a stick
Makes me sick
Makes my tummy go
Two forty-six
Not because it's dirty
Not because it's clean
Not because I kissed my momma
Behind the magazines
Girls, girls
Do you want to fight?
Here come Dickey
With her pants on tight
She can wiggle
She can woggle
She can do all that
I bet you ten dollars
You can't do this
Count to ten with your eyes closed
A-baby one
A-baby two
A-baby three, four, five
Baby, I don't take no little jive
A-baby six
A-baby seven
A-baby eight, nine, ten
You better back it up and do it again

I wish I had a nickel
I wish I had a dime
I wish I had a boyfriend
Who kissed me all the time
My momma took my nickel
My daddy took my dime
My sister took my boyfriend
And gave me Frankenstein
He made me wash the windows
He made me wash the floor
He made me wash his underwear
And he kicked me out the door

Super Superstar
Hey
Akira is my name
Superstar
Kickball is my game
Winning on my mind
Hey
Scorpio is my number one sign
Super Superstar
Hey

Super Superstar
Hey
Nathalee is my name
Basketball is my game
Winning on my mind
Hey
Leo is my number one sign
Super Superstar
Hey

Hula hula
Now who think they bad
Hula hula
Now who think they bad
I think I'm bad
'Cause Acie my name
And toys is my game
Take a sip of my potion
And dance in slow motion
Uh-huh
She think she bad
Baby baby don't make me mad
Uh-huh
She think she cool
Baby baby don't act a fool
Uh-huh
She think she sweet
Sweetest person you ever meet
Uh-huh
She think she fine
Baby baby I'll blow your mind

Hollywood rock swinging
Hollywood rock swinging
My name is Aniesha
I'm number one
My reputation is having fun
So if you see me just step aside
'Cause mighty Aniesha don't take no jive

Hollywood rock swinging
Hollywood rock swinging
My name is Katrina
I'm number two
My reputation is me and you
So if you see me just step on back
'Cause mighty Katrina don't take no slack

Hollywood rock swinging
Hollywood rock swinging
My name is Natasha
I'm number twelve
My reputation is ringing that bell
So if you see me just step aside
'Cause mighty Natasha don't take no jive

Little Sally Walker
Sitting in the saucer
Rise, Sally, Rise
Wipe your weepy eyes
And put your hands on your hips
And make your backbone slip
Oh, shake it to the east
Oh, shake it to the west
Oh, shake it to the very one
    that you love the best
Turn to the east
Turn to the west
Turn to the very one
    that you love the best

I was born in a frying pan
Just to see how old I am
Is a one, two, three, four, five (until you miss)

Shake shake shake
Eeny meeny
That's a queeny
Ooh ba Thumbelina
Ah cha ca che Liberace
Oh baby I love you
Yes I do
Take a peach
Take a plum
Take a piece of bubble gum
No peach
No plum
Just a piece of bubble gum
Oooshe ahshe
Oooshe ahshe
I want a piece of pie
The pie too sweet
I want a piece of meat
The meat too tough
I want to ride the bus
The bus too full
I want to ride the bull
The bull too black
I want my money back
The money too green
I want a diamond ring

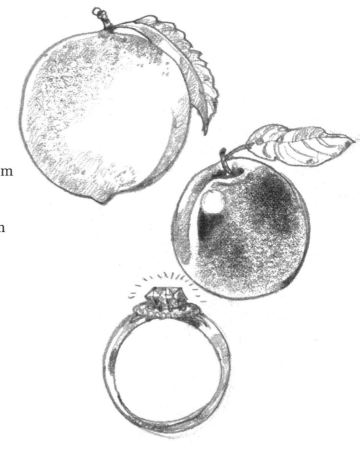

Teddy Bear, Teddy Bear
Turn around
Teddy Bear, Teddy Bear
Touch the ground
Teddy Bear, Teddy Bear
Shine your shoes
Teddy Bear, Teddy Bear
That will do
Teddy Bear, Teddy Bear
Go upstairs
Teddy Bear, Teddy Bear
Say your prayers
Teddy Bear, Teddy Bear
Turn off the light
Teddy Bear, Teddy Bear
Say good night

Vaccination
Education
Does it hurt
Or does it sting
It don't hurt or anything

(Jump rope going through the grades starting
with kindergarten. If you're hit by the rope,
that's a spanking and you have to repeat a grade.)

Cinderella
Went downtown
To kiss her fellow
How many kisses did she get?
She got one, two, three, four, five, six

Ice cream soda water
Cream on the top
Show me the initials
Of your honeybunch
A B C D E F G H

Bubble gum bubble gum
In my mouth
How many pieces do you wish
One, two, three, four, five
A-six, seven, eight, nine, ten

This the way you will a be
Will a be will a be
This the way you will a be
All night long

Oh step back Sally
Sally Sally
Oh step back Sally
All night long

Oh walking through the alley
Alley alley
Walking through the alley
All night long

Oh here comes Sally
Sally Sally
Here comes Sally
All night long

Oh here comes another one
Just like the other one
Here comes another one
All night long

This the way you will a be
Will a be will a be
This the way you will a be
All night long

Hey girl
Whatcha got
Soda pop
Gimme some
Uh-huh
Buy you some

Hey brother
Whatcha got
Soda pop
Gimme some
Uh-huh
Buy you some

Hey sister
Whatcha got
Soda pop
Gimme some
Uh-huh
Buy you some

Hey mother

Hey uncle

My momma and your momma
Lives across the street
Eighteen nineteen German Street
Every night they have a fight
And this is what they say
Boys are rotten
Just like cotton
Girls are handy
Just like candy

Eat a piece of candy
Greedy greedy
Jump out the window
Crazy crazy
Don't wash the dishes
Lazy lazy

23

24

White white
You're light as a kite

Brown brown
You're a clown

Green green
You're mean

Blue blue
You've got the flu
I don't want to play with you

White white
You're getting married tonight

Pink pink
You stink

One two three
Bumble bee
You forgot to brush your teeth
I don't care
Baby bear
You forgot your underwear

V-I-C-T-O-R-Y
V-I-C-T-O-R-Y
Down the road there's a cemetery
Down the road there's a cemetery
That's where the Jaycees gonna get buried
That's where the Jaycees gonna get buried
Umph get down
Umph umph get down
Umph get down
Umph umph get down

Peace
O.K.
I don't play
These too many (five fingers)
This too skinny (little finger)
This too fat (clenched fist)
Now you take that

Deshawn had a baby
Pizza Pizza Daddy O
What's his name?
Pizza Pizza Daddy O
Jesse James
Pizza Pizza Daddy O
What it look like?
Pizza Pizza Daddy O
Like a monkey
Pizza Pizza Daddy O
Do the monkey
Pizza Pizza Daddy O
Do the jerk
Pizza Pizza Daddy O
Who do you choose?
Pizza Pizza Daddy O

Hey little girl with dippity do
Your mom's got the measles
And your daddy do too
Take a ABCDEFG
Take a HIJKLMNOP
Take a booster shot
Take a booster shot
And freeze

When I count to one
Do the rock with me
I say
Cha cha boom
Cha cha boom
That's what I say

When I count to two
Do the flower with me
I say
Cha cha boom
Cha cha boom
That's what I say

When I count to three
Do the spank with me
I say
Cha cha boom
Cha cha boom
That's what I say

Miss Mary Mack Mack Mack
All dressed in black black black
With silver buttons buttons buttons
All down her back back back
She asked her mother mother mother
For fifteen cents cents cents
To see the elephant elephant elephant
Jump the fence fence fence
He jumped so high high high
He touched the sky sky sky
And never came back
'Til the fourth of July-ly-ly

Old lady Dinah Dinah Dinah
Sick in the bed bed bed
Sent for the doctor doctor doctor
And the doctor said said said
Now get up Dinah Dinah Dinah
You ain't sick sick sick
All you need need need
Is a hickory stick stick stick

Uncle Ed Ed Ed
Fell out of bed bed bed
Bust his head head head
On a piece of corn bread bread bread
Corn bread rough rough rough
Biscuits tough tough tough
Never had enough-nough-nough
Of that good old stuff stuff stuff

July third third third
July fourth fourth fourth
July the eighth eighth eighth
A knife and a fork fork fork

31

I like coffee
I like tea
I like a little boy
And he likes me
Little boy, little boy
Don't you cry
I've got another boy on my mind
Step back Jack
Your hands too black
To the front
To the back
To the side by side
To the front
To the back
To the side by side
The president's got a hole in his underwear

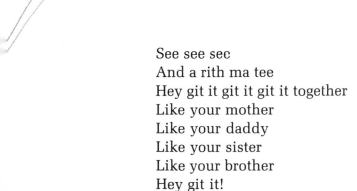

See see sec
And a rith ma tee
Hey git it git it git it together
Like your mother
Like your daddy
Like your sister
Like your brother
Hey git it!

Knock knock
Who's there
Cougar's knocking everywhere
Knock knock
Hey hey
Knock knock
My name is BeVona
Up above me
Hey
I see some love
Hey
I see some love
Hey
She see some love
One, two, three, four
Come on girls
Get off that floor

Jingle bells
Batman smells
Robin laid an egg
Batmobile lost a wheel
And Joker got away

Banana
Bump bump banana
My name is Alfreda
Banana
Bump bump banana
We like to race
Banana
Bump bump banana
Hey
I got rhythm
I got soul
I got something Toysha can't have
Banana
Bump bump banana

Jim Black
Jim Black
Blacker than coal
Talk more stuff than a radio

Here come Mr. Willy
Walking down the hall
Eating fuzzy-wuzzy
All night long

35

Miss Sue, Miss Sue
Miss Sue from Alabama
Here she come with a hickory stick
Uh-huh
Uh-huh
Here she come with a hickory stick
Uh-huh
Uh-huh
Hey Dishelle
Somebody's calling your name
Hey Dishelle
Somebody's playing your game
Hey Dishelle
Somebody wants you on the telephone
If it ain't my man
Tell him I ain't home
Sitting at the table
Chopping up potatoes
Waiting for the clock to go
Chock a boo
Chock a boo
She say wishy washy
She say wishy washy
boom

When I was a baby, a baby, a baby
This is what I'd do
Hmm, hmm, hmm hmm hmm (sucking thumb)
All day long
All day long

When I was a girl, a girl, a girl
This is what I'd do
Uh-huh, hum hum hum (jumping rope)
All day long
All day long

When I was a teenager, a teenager, a teenager
This is what I'd do
Mmm hem, priss priss priss (hands on hips, prancing)
All day long
All day long

When I was a lady, a lady, a lady
This is what I'd do
Shooo, shooo, shoo shoo shoo (spray perfume behind ears)
All day long
All day long

When I was a teacher, a teacher, a teacher
This is what I'd do
Uh-huh, tst tst tst (pointing finger)
All day long
All day long

When I got married, married, married
This is what I'd do
Smack, smack, smooch smooch smooch (kissing the air)
All day long
All day long

When my husband got beat up, beat up, beat up
This is what I'd do
Ah boom, ah boom, ah boom boom boom (shadow boxing)
All day long
All day long

When my baby die, die, die
This is what I'd do
Boo hoo, boo hoo, boo hoo (wiping tears from eyes)
All day long
All day long

When I die, die, die
This is what I'd do
Oooooooooooooh (All fall down)

I don't want to go to college
Anymore more more
There's a big fat policeman
At the door door door
He'll pull you by the collar
Make you pay a dollar
See what I mean
Jelly bean
Wash your face with gasoline
Jump in a lake
Swallow a snake
Come back home with a tummy ache

Abraham Lincoln was a good ole man
Jumped out the window with a stick
    in his hand

Happy birthday to you
You live in the zoo
You smell like a monkey
And look like one too

Down down baby
Down down the roller coaster
Shoe shine baby
Shoe shine the roller coaster
She's so good to me
Down down baby
Down down the roller coaster
Sweet sweet baby
Please don't you let me go
Shimmy shimmy cocopuffs
Shimmy shimmy pow
Shimmy shimmy cocopuffs
Shimmy shimmy pow

Down by the river
Down by the sea
Johnny broke a bottle
And blamed it on me
I told Mama
Mama told Papa
Papa gave Johnny some H-O-T

41

My name is Yserdia
I was sitting in a tree
I fell down and broke my neck
And that was the end of me
My mama called the doctor
He took me in the house
He laid me in a bed
And I saw a little mouse
The mouse jumped on my bed
And scared me half to death
My mama came in the room
And told me his name was Beth

You missed me
You missed me
Now you gotta kiss me
You jumped to Colorado
And then you caught me
You caught me
You caught me

Forget you
Forgot you
I never thought about you
Give me a piece of paper
And I'll write all about you

S. O.
I say no

My mama
Your mama
Hanging out clothes
My mama sock your mama
In the nose
Did it hurt?

I have a boyfriend
Nabisco
He's so sweet
Nabisco
Like a cherry tree
Nabisco
Ahche ahche and a boom de boom
I need some money
And I need it soon
So let's get the rhythm of the hands
Clap clap
Now we've got the rhythm of the hands
Clap clap
Now let's get the rhythm of the feet
Stomp stomp
Now we've got the rhythm of the feet
Stomp stomp
Now let's get the rhythm of the head
Ding dong
Now we've got the rhythm of the head
Ding dong
Now let's get the rhythm of the hips
Hot dog
Now we've got the rhythm of the hips
Hot dog
Now let's get the rhythm of Nabisco
Clap clap
Stomp stomp
Ding dong
Hot dog
Now we've got the rhythm of Nabisco
Hot dog!

If you don't get out de way
I'll kick you out de way

So
So
Back back back to you

Look up
Look down
Look all around
Your pants are falling down

So so
Your draws are to'

Shut don't go up
Prices do
A monkey like you
Belongs in the zoo

Shut don't go up
Prices do
Take my advice
And shut up too

Oh, sailor went to sea sea sea
To see what he could see see see
That all that he could see see see
Was the bottom of the big blue sea sea sea

Oh, sailor went to chop chop chop
To see what he could chop chop chop
That all that he could chop chop chop
Was the bottom of the big blue chop chop chop

Oh, sailor went to ooh washy wash
To see what he could ooh washy wash
That all that he could ooh washy wash
Was the bottom of the big blue ooh washy wash

Oh, sailor went to China
To see what he could China
But all that he could China
Was the bottom of the big blue China

Oh, sailor went to sea sea sea
Chop chop chop
Ooh washy wash
China
To see what he could see see see
Chop chop chop
Ooh washy wash
China
That all that he could see see see
Chop chop chop
Ooh washy wash
China
Was the bottom of the big blue sea sea sea
Chop chop chop
Ooh washy wash
China

One two
Buckle my shoe
Three four
Knock on the door
Five six
Pick up sticks
Seven eight
Lay them straight
Nine ten
A big bad hen
Eleven twelve
Dig in there
Thirteen fourteen
Make some kissing
Sixteen seventeen
Clean up the kitchen

INDEX OF FIRST LINES

j808.1
A64

10.95
C.3

Afro-American

Detroit City Ordinance 29-85, Section
29-2-2(b) provides: "Any person who
retains any library material or any part
thereof for more than fifty (50) cal-
endar days beyond the due date shall
be guilty of a misdemeanor."

Duffield Branch Library
2507 W. Grand Blvd.
DETROIT, PUBLIC LIBRARY
Detroit, Michigan 48208

The number of books that may be
drawn at one time by the card holder
is governed by the reasonable needs of
the reader and the material on hand.
Books for junior readers are subject
to special rules.